*The Rose Window
and Other Verse from
New Poems*

Also Available:

Odes to Common Things by Pablo Neruda
Odes to Opposites by Pablo Neruda

RAINER MARIA RILKE

The Rose Window

and Other Verse from
New Poems

Selected and Illustrated by Ferris Cook

A Bulfinch Press Book | Little, Brown and Company

BOSTON · NEW YORK · TORONTO · LONDON

Ferris Cook gratefully acknowledges the contributions of the translators:

Stephen Cohn

Richard Exner

Albert Ernest Flemming

J. B. Leishman

C. F. MacIntyre

Stephen Mitchell

M. D. Herter Norton

Edward Snow

Franz Wright

First Edition

LIBRARY OF CONGRESS CATALOGING-IN-PUBLICATION DATA

Rilke, Rainer Maria, 1875–1926.

    [Neue Gedichte. English & German. Selections]

    The rose window and other verse from New Poems / selected and illustrated by Ferris Cook.

       p.   cm.

    "A Bulfinch Press book."

    English and German.

    ISBN 0-8212-2364-X

    1. Rilke, Rainer Maria, 1875–1926—Translations into English.

  I. Cook, Ferris. II. Title.

PT2635.I65R3813   1997

831'.912—dc21   97–26948

Bulfinch Press is an imprint and trademark of Little, Brown and Company (Inc.)
Published simultaneously in Canada by Little, Brown & Company (Canada) Limited

PRINTED IN THE UNITED STATES OF AMERICA

For Ken

Inhalt

Contents

BUCH 2

BOOK 2

Rainer Maria Rilke was born in 1875 in Prague and died in 1926 in Switzerland. Rilke developed a rich poetic style characterized by striking symbolism and visual imagery, and is generally regarded as the greatest lyric poet of modern Germany. Most of *New Poems* was written in Paris, where Rilke admired, and was influenced by, Rodin.

The Rose Window and Other Verse from New Poems is a selection of poetry taken from *New Poems*, published in two parts: the first in December 1907 and the second in August 1908.

BUCH 1 | BOOK 1

Früher Apollo

Wie manches Mal durch das noch unbelaubte
Gezweig ein Morgen durchsieht, der schon ganz
im Frühling ist: so ist in seinem Haupte
nichts was verhindern könnte, daß der Glanz

aller Gedichte uns fast tödlich träfe;
denn noch kein Schatten ist in seinem Schaun,
zu kühl für Lorbeer sind noch seine Schläfe
und später erst wird aus den Augenbraun

hochstämmig sich der Rosengarten heben,
aus welchem Blätter, einzeln, ausgelöst
hintreiben werden auf des Mundes Beben,

der jetzt noch still ist, niegebraucht und blinkend
und nur mit seinem Lächeln etwas trinkend
als würde ihm sein Singen eingeflößt.

Early Apollo

As when sometimes through branches, leafless still,
a morning bursts with all the force of Spring,
so there is nothing in his head that could
prevent the radiant power of all poems

to strike us almost deadly with its light.
For there is yet no shadow in his gaze,
too cool for laurel are his temples still,
and round the eyebrows only later will

come climbing long-stemmed roses from his garden,
and petals, separating from their blooms,
will drift and rest upon his trembling mouth

that yet is silent, sparkling and unused,
and only hinting with a smile as if
a song were soon to reach his open lips.

Grabmal eines jungen Mädchens

Wir gedenkens noch. Das ist, als müßte
alles dieses einmal wieder sein.
Wie ein Baum an der Limonenküste
trugst du deine kleinen leichten Brüste
in das Rauschen seines Bluts hinein:

— jenes Gottes.
       Und es war der schlanke
Flüchtling, der Verwöhnende der Fraun.
Süß und glühend, warm wie dein Gedanke,
überschattend deine frühe Flanke
und geneigt wie deine Augenbraun.

Epitaph for a Young Girl

We still remember, for it is as if
a time must come when all will be renewed.
Like a tree growing among lemon-groves
you offered up the brightness of your breasts
which he took deep into his singing blood.

Did you not recognise that slippery god,
the pleasurer of women and their joy?
As sweet, as ardent as your own desires
he cast his shadow on your youthfulness,
curved over you, as slender as a bow.

Pietà

So seh ich, Jesus, deine Füße wieder,
die damals eines Jünglings Füße waren,
da ich sie bang entkleidete und wusch;
wie standen sie verwirrt in meinen Haaren
und wie ein weißes Wild im Dornenbusch.

So seh ich deine niegeliebten Glieder
zum erstenmal in dieser Liebesnacht.
Wir legten uns noch nie zusammen nieder,
und nun wird nur bewundert und gewacht.

Doch, siehe, deine Hände sind zerrissen—:
Geliebter, nicht von mir, von meinen Bissen.
Dein Herz steht offen und man kann hinein:
das hätte dürfen nur mein Eingang sein.

Nun bist du müde, und dein müder Mund
hat keine Lust zu meinem wehen Munde—.
O Jesus, Jesus, wann war unsre Stunde?
Wie gehn wir beide wunderlich zugrund.

Pietà

Again, Lord, for a second time I know
the feet I touched when you and they were young.
I washed their dust away and saw them shine
like shy white creatures, caught and held among
my tumbled hair as if ensnared by thorns.

Again I see your limbs that never knew
their lover's touch; tonight I hold them fast.
Craving you always, I may hold you now.
Amazed, awake, I lie with you at last.

Your heart stands open. Any may go in
where there should be a place for me alone.
And, see! your wounded hands, far better they
had felt the sharpness of my teeth in play.

I feel your weariness. Your weary mouth
feels no desire for my grieving mouth.
How strange a way for us to meet our end!
Lord, could no time, no place for us be found?

Der Tod des Dichters

Er lag. Sein aufgestelltes Antlitz war
bleich und verweigernd in den steilen Kissen,
seitdem die Welt und dieses von-ihr-Wissen,
von seinen Sinnen abgerissen,
zurückfiel an das teilnahmslose Jahr.

Die, so ihn leben sahen, wußten nicht,
wie sehr er Eines war mit allem diesen;
denn Dieses: diese Tiefen, diese Wiesen
und diese Wasser *waren* sein Gesicht.

O sein Gesicht war diese ganze Weite,
die jetzt noch zu ihm will und um ihn wirbt;
und seine Maske, die nun bang verstirbt,
ist zart und offen wie die Innenseite
von einer Frucht, die an der Luft verdirbt.

The Poet's Death

He lay. His erected countenance was
pale and refusing in the steep pillows,
now that the world and this knowledge
of it, ripped away from his senses,
had fallen back to the indifferent year.

Those who saw him living didn't know
how completely one he was with all of this;
for this: these meadows, these valleys
and these waters *were* his face.

O his face was this entire expanse,
that now still seeks him and tries to woo him;
and his mask, which now fearfully dies,
is tender and open, like the inside
of a piece of fruit that spoils in the air.

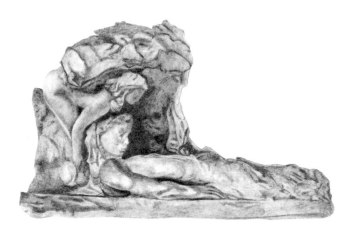

Buddha

Als ob er horchte. Stille: eine Ferne ...
Wir halten ein und hören sie nicht mehr.
Und er ist Stern. Und andre große Sterne,
die wir nicht sehen, stehen um ihn her.

O er ist Alles. Wirklich, warten wir,
daß er uns sähe? Sollte er bedürfen?
Und wenn wir hier uns vor ihm niederwürfen,
er bliebe tief und träge wie ein Tier.

Denn das, was uns zu seinen Füßen reißt,
das kreist in ihm seit Millionen Jahren.
Er, der vergißt was wir erfahren
und der erfährt was uns verweist.

Buddha

As though he listened. Stillness: something far . . .
We hold our breath; our hearing, though, 's too dim.
And he is star. And many a mighty star,
beyond our vision, is attending him.

Oh, he is all. Lingering, have we the least
hope that he'll notice? Could he ever need?
And if we fell before him here to plead,
he'd still sit deep and idle as a beast.

For that in him which drags us to his feet
has circled in him for a million years.
He who forgets our hopes and fears
in thoughts from which our thoughts retreat.

L'Ange du Méridien
Chartres

Im Sturm, der um die starke Kathedrale
wie ein Verneiner stürzt der denkt und denkt,
fühlt man sich zärtlicher mit einem Male
von deinem Lächeln zu dir hingelenkt:

lächelnder Engel, fühlende Figur,
mit einem Mund, gemacht aus hundert Munden:
gewahrst du gar nicht, wie dir unsre Stunden
abgleiten von der vollen Sonnenuhr,

auf der des Tages ganze Zahl zugleich,
gleich wirklich, steht in tiefem Gleichgewichte,
als wären alle Stunden reif und reich.

Was weißt du, Steinerner, von unserm Sein?
und hältst du mit noch seligerm Gesichte
vielleicht die Tafel in die Nacht hinein?

The Angel of the Meridian
(Chartres Cathedral)

Amidst the storm that round the great cathedral
rages like an atheist who thinks and thinks,
we suddenly are drawn with tender feelings
toward your smiling countenance among the saints.

Beguiling angel, sympathetic statue,
with mouth as fashioned from a hundred mouths:
are you aware how from your full sundial
our hours keep gliding past into oblivion

as do our days like a procession, measured
equally by your dial's impartial balancing,
as if each hour and day had reached full ripeness.

What do you know, stone angel, of our being?
And does your blessed face increase in radiance
as you uphold the sundial out into the night?

Die Kathedrale

In jenen kleinen Städten, wo herum
die alten Häuser wie ein Jahrmarkt hocken,
der *sie* bemerkt hat plötzlich und, erschrocken,
die Buden zumacht und, ganz zu und stumm,

die Schreier still, die Trommeln angehalten,
zu ihr hinaufhorcht aufgeregten Ohrs —:
dieweil sie ruhig immer in dem alten
Faltenmantel ihrer Contreforts
dasteht und von den Häusern gar nicht weiß:

in jenen kleinen Städten kannst du sehn,
wie sehr entwachsen ihrem Umgangskreis
die Kathedralen waren. Ihr Erstehn
ging über alles fort, so wie den Blick
des eignen Lebens viel zu große Nähe
fortwährend übersteigt, und als geschähe
nichts anderes; als wäre Das Geschick,
was sich in ihnen aufhäuft ohne Maßen,
versteinert und zum Dauernden bestimmt,
nicht Das, was unten in den dunkeln Straßen
vom Zufall irgendwelche Namen nimmt
und darin geht, wie Kinder Grün und Rot
und was der Krämer hat als Schürze tragen.
Da war Geburt in diesen Unterlagen,
und Kraft und Andrang war in diesem Ragen
und Liebe überall wie Wein und Brot,
und die Portale voller Liebesklagen.
Das Leben zögerte im Stundenschlagen,
und in den Türmen, welche voll Entsagen
auf einmal nicht mehr stiegen, war der Tod.

The Cathedral

In those small towns where, clustered round about,
old houses squat and jostle like a fair,
that's just caught sight of *it*, and then and there
shut up the stalls, and, silenced every shout,

the criers still, the drum-sticks all suspended,
stands gazing up at it with straining ears:
while it, as calm as ever, in the splendid
wrinkled buttress-mantle rears
itself above the homes it never knew:

in those small towns you come to realise
how the cathedrals utterly outgrew
their whole environment. Their birth and rise,
as our own life's too great proximity
will mount beyond our vision and our sense
of other happenings, took precedence
of all things; as though that were history,
piled up in their immeasurable masses
in petrification safe from circumstance,
not that, which down among the dark streets passes
and takes whatever name is given by chance
and goes in that, as children green or red,
or what the dealer has, wear in rotation.
For birth was here, within this deep foundation,
and strength and purpose in this aspiration,
and love, like bread and wine, was all around,
and porches full of lovers' lamentation.
In the tolled hours was heard life's hesitation,
and in those towers that, full of resignation,
ceased all at once from climbing, death was found.

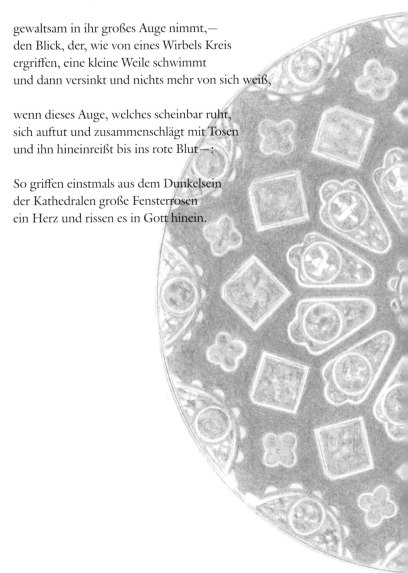

Die Fensterrose

Da drin: das träge Treten ihrer Tatzen
macht eine Stille, die dich fast verwirrt;
und wie dann plötzlich eine von den Katzen
den Blick an ihr, der hin und wieder irrt,

gewaltsam in ihr großes Auge nimmt,—
den Blick, der, wie von eines Wirbels Kreis
ergriffen, eine kleine Weile schwimmt
und dann versinkt und nichts mehr von sich weiß,

wenn dieses Auge, welches scheinbar ruht,
sich auftut und zusammenschlägt mit Tosen
und ihn hineinreißt bis ins rote Blut—:

So griffen einstmals aus dem Dunkelsein
der Kathedralen große Fensterrosen
ein Herz und rissen es in Gott hinein.

The Rose Window

Inside, the lazy padding of soft feet
creates a silence, almost stupefies;
then all at once one of the drowsing cats
awakes — and pounces; its enormous eye

seizes the drifting image of that quiet,
which for a little while yet swims around,
before the golden whirlpool sucks at it
and drags it down into oblivion:

just as this eye apparently asleep
gapes open, strikes, and drags its capture deep
into the thunder of its own red blood —

so the rose window in that holy time
within the great cathedral's scented gloom
captured a heart and dragged it up to God.

Gott im Mittelalter

Und sie hatten Ihn in sich erspart
und sie wollten, daß er sei und richte,
und sie hängten schließlich wie Gewichte
(zu verhindern seine Himmelfahrt)

an ihn ihrer großen Kathedralen
Last und Masse. Und er sollte nur
über seine grenzenlosen Zahlen
zeigend kreisen und wie eine Uhr

Zeichen geben ihrem Tun und Tagwerk.
Aber plötzlich kam er ganz in Gang,
und die Leute der entsetzten Stadt

ließen ihn, vor seiner Stimme bang,
weitergehn mit ausgehängtem Schlagwerk
und entflohn vor seinem Zifferblatt.

God in the Middle Ages

And they'd stored him up inside themselves
and they wanted him to be and reign
and finally (to hinder his ascension)
they loaded the cargo and ballast

of their great cathedrals on him.
All he had to do
was move around his limitless numerals
pointing, and like a clock regulate

their work and other daily occupations.
But all at once he started striking
and the people, terrified

by his voice, left him
with his inner mechanisms showing,
and fled before his face.

Morgue

Da liegen sie bereit, als ob es gälte,
nachträglich eine Handlung zu erfinden,
die mit einander und mit dieser Kälte
sie zu versöhnen weiß und zu verbinden;

denn das ist alles noch wie ohne Schluß.
Wasfür ein Name hätte in den Taschen
sich finden sollen? An dem Überdruß
um ihren Mund hat man herumgewaschen:

er ging nicht ab; er wurde nur ganz rein.
Die Bärte stehen, noch ein wenig härter,
doch ordentlicher im Geschmack der Wärter,

nur um die Gaffenden nicht anzuwidern.
Die Augen haben hinter ihren Lidern
sich umgewandt und schauen jetzt hinein.

Morgue

Here they lie ready, as though what were still
needful were that some action be invented
whereby with one another and this chill
they might become united and contented;

for all is still as though without conclusion.
What names, we'd like to know, may have been found
inside their pockets? All the disillusion
about their mouths has been washed round and round

it didn't go; it merely came quite clean.
Their beards are left them, just a bit less pendant,
but tidier, as it seems to the attendant,

so that the starers shan't be disconcerted.
The eyes beneath their eyelids have averted
their gaze from outwardness to that within.

Der Panther

Im Jardin des Plantes, Paris

Sein Blick ist vom Vorübergehn der Stäbe
so müd geworden, daß er nichts mehr hält.
Ihm ist, als ob es tausend Stäbe gäbe
und hinter tausend Stäben keine Welt.

Der weiche Gang geschmeidig starker Schritte,
der sich im allerkleinsten Kreise dreht,
ist wie ein Tanz von Kraft um eine Mitte,
in der betäubt ein großer Wille steht.

Nur manchmal schiebt der Vorhang der Pupille
sich lautlos auf —. Dann geht ein Bild hinein,
geht durch der Glieder angespannte Stille —
und hört im Herzen auf zu sein.

The Panther
In the Jardin des Plantes, Paris

Ceaselessly the bars and rails keep passing
Till his gaze, from weariness, lets all things go. For
it seems to him the world consists of bars and
railings and beyond them world exists no more.

Supple, strong, elastic is his pacing
and its circles much too narrow for a leap,
like a dance of strength around a middle
where a mighty will was put to sleep.

Yet from time to time the pupil's curtain
rises silently. An image enters, flies
through the limbs' intensive stillness
until, entering the very heart, it dies.

Die Gazelle
Gazella Dorcas

Verzauberte: wie kann der Einklang zweier
erwählter Worte je den Reim erreichen,
der in dir kommt und geht, wie auf ein Zeichen.
Aus deiner Stirne steigen Laub und Leier,

und alles Deine geht schon im Vergleich
durch Liebeslieder, deren Worte, weich
wie Rosenblätter, dem, der nicht mehr liest,
sich auf die Augen legen, die er schließt:

um dich zu sehen: hingetragen, als
wäre mit Sprüngen jeder Lauf geladen
und schösse nur nicht ab, solang der Hals

das Haupt ins Horchen hält: wie wenn beim Baden
im Wald die Badende sich unterbricht:
den Waldsee im gewendeten Gesicht.

The Gazelle
Dorcas Gazelle

Enchanted one: how shall two chosen words
achieve the harmony of the pure rhyme
which in you like a signal comes and goes?
From your forehead the leafy lyre climbs,

and all your being moves in sure accord,
like those love-lyrics whose words softly flow:
rose petals laid upon the closed eyelids
of one grown weary, who no longer reads

but shuts his eyes to see you — swiftly brought,
as though each leg were charged with leaps but not
fired, as long as the neck holds the head

quiet to listen: as when in a green place
a bather in the woods is interrupted . . .
with the lake's shine on her averted face.

Das Einhorn

Der Heilige hob das Haupt, und das Gebet
fiel wie ein Helm zurück von seinem Haupte:
denn lautlos nahte sich das niegeglaubte,
das weiße Tier, das wie eine geraubte
hülflose Hindin mit den Augen fleht.

Der Beine elfenbeinernes Gestell
bewegte sich in leichten Gleichgewichten,
ein weißer Glanz glitt selig durch das Fell,
und auf der Tierstirn, auf der stillen, lichten,
stand, wie ein Turm im Mond, das Horn so hell,
und jeder Schritt geschah, es aufzurichten.

Das Maul mit seinem rosagrauen Flaum
war leicht gerafft, so daß ein wenig Weiß
(weißer als alles) von den Zähnen glänzte;
die Nüstern nahmen auf und lechzten leis.
Doch seine Blicke, die kein Ding begrenzte,
warfen sich Bilder in den Raum
und schlossen einen blauen Sagenkreis.

The Unicorn

And then the saint looked up, and in surprise
the prayer fell like a helmet from his head:
for softly neared that never-credited
white creature, which, like some unparented,
some helpless hind, beseeches with its eyes.

The ivory framework of the limbs so light
moved like a pair of balances deflected,
there glided through the coat a gleam of white,
and on the forehead, where the beams collected,
stood, like a moon-lit tower, the horn so bright,
at every footstep proudly re-erected.

Its mouth was slightly open, and a trace
of white through the soft down of grey and rose
(whitest of whites) came from the gleaming teeth;
its nostrils panted gently for repose.
Its gaze, though, checked by nothing here beneath,
projecting pictures into space,
brought a blue saga-cycle to a close.

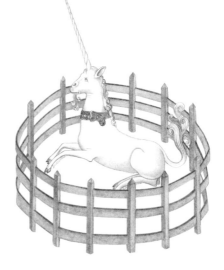

Sankt Sebastian

Wie ein Liegender so steht er; ganz
hingehalten von dem großen Willen.
Weitentrückt wie Mütter, wenn sie stillen,
und in sich gebunden wie ein Kranz.

Und die Pfeile kommen: jetzt und jetzt
und als sprängen sie aus seinen Lenden,
eisern bebend mit den freien Enden.
Doch er lächelt dunkel, unverletzt.

Einmal nur wird seine Trauer groß,
und die Augen liegen schmerzlich bloß,
bis sie etwas leugnen, wie Geringes,
und als ließen sie verächtlich los
die Vernichter eines schönen Dinges.

Saint Sebastian

He stands like a man reclining — completely
held up there by a magnificent choice. Withdrawn
and self-possessed, like mothers when they nurse,
and involved in himself, like a wreath.

And the arrows arrive: now, and now,
as if they were springing from his groin,
shuddering stiffly at the feathered ends.
Yet he just smiles darkly, undamaged.

Only at one point does his sorrow grow
pronounced, the eyes in naked pain, until
they seem to turn aside from something futile;
as if dismissing with utter contempt
the destroyers of beautiful things.

Römische Sarkophage

Was aber hindert uns zu glauben, daß
(so wie wir hingestellt sind und verteilt)
nicht eine kleine Zeit nur Drang und Haß
und dies Verwirrende in uns verweilt,

wie einst in dem verzierten Sarkophag
bei Ringen, Götterbildern, Gläsern, Bändern,
in langsam sich verzehrenden Gewändern
ein langsam Aufgelöstes lag —

bis es die unbekannten Munde schluckten,
die niemals reden. (Wo besteht und denkt
ein Hirn, um ihrer einst sich zu bedienen?)

Da wurde von den alten Aquädukten
ewiges Wasser in sie eingelenkt — :
das spiegelt jetzt und geht und glänzt in ihnen.

Roman Sarcophagi

Why should we too, though, not anticipate
(set down here and assigned our places thus)
that only for a short time rage and hate
and this bewildering will remain in us,

as in the ornate sarcophagus, enclosed
with images of gods, rings, glasses, trappings,
there lay in slowly self-consuming wrappings
something being slowly decomposed —

till swallowed by those unknown mouths at last,
that never speak. (Where bides a brain that may
yet trust the utterance of its thinking to them?)

Then from the ancient aqueducts there passed
eternal water into them one day: —
that mirrors now and moves and sparkles through them.

Der Schwan

Diese Mühsal, durch noch Ungetanes
schwer und wie gebunden hinzugehn,
gleicht dem ungeschaffnen Gang des Schwanes.

Und das Sterben, dieses Nichtmehrfassen
jenes Grunds, auf dem wir täglich stehn,
seinem ängstlichen Sich-Niederlassen—:

in die Wasser, die ihn sanft empfangen
und die sich, wie glücklich und vergangen,
unter ihm zurückziehn, Flut um Flut;
während er unendlich still und sicher
immer mündiger und königlicher
und gelassener zu ziehn geruht.

The Swan

This misery that through the still-undone
must pass, bound and heavily weighed down,
is like the awkward walking of the swan.

And death, where we no longer comprehend
the very ground on which we daily stand,
is like his anxious letting-himself-go

into the water, soft against his breast,
which now how easily together flows
behind him in a little wake of waves . . .
while he, infinitely silent, self-possessed,
and ever more mature, is pleased to move
serenely on in his majestic way.

Der Dichter

Du entfernst dich von mir, du Stunde.
Wunden schlägt mir dein Flügelschlag.
Allein: was soll ich mit meinem Munde?
mit meiner Nacht? mit meinem Tag?

Ich habe keine Geliebte, kein Haus,
keine Stelle auf der ich lebe.
Alle Dinge, an die ich mich gebe,
werden reich und geben mich aus.

The Poet

Fugitive moment! how fast you escape me:
how you can wound with each stroke of your wing!
All alone? then what was I given my tongue for;
why was I given these nights, or these days?

I have no particular place here,
no beloved, no house of my own.
Though I enrich every thing that I enter,
enriched, it will easily spend me again.

Tanagra

Ein wenig gebrannter Erde,
wie von großer Sonne gebrannt.
Als wäre die Gebärde
einer Mädchenhand
auf einmal nicht mehr vergangen;
ohne nach etwas zu langen,
zu keinem Dinge hin
aus ihrem Gefühle führend,
nur an sich selber rührend
wie eine Hand ans Kinn.

Wir heben und wir drehen
eine und eine Figur;
wir können fast verstehen
weshalb sie nicht vergehen, —
aber wir sollen nur
tiefer und wunderbarer
hängen an dem was war
und lächeln: ein wenig klarer
vielleicht als vor einem Jahr.

Tanagra

A bit of baked earth,
baked as by a mighty sun.
As if the gesture
that a girl's hand makes
had suddenly remained:
without reaching for anything,
leading from its feeling
toward no object,
only touching itself
like a hand raised to a chin.

We lift and we keep turning
the same few figures;
we can almost understand
why they don't perish,—
but we're meant only
more deeply and wonderingly
to cling to what once was
and smile: a bit more clearly
perhaps than a year before.

Die Erblindende

Sie saß so wie die anderen beim Tee.
Mir war zuerst, als ob sie ihre Tasse
ein wenig anders als die andern fasse.
Sie lächelte einmal. Es tat fast weh.

Und als man schließlich sich erhob und sprach
und langsam und wie es der Zufall brachte
durch viele Zimmer ging (man sprach und lachte),
da sah ich sie. Sie ging den andern nach,

verhalten, so wie eine, welche gleich
wird singen müssen und vor vielen Leuten;
auf ihren hellen Augen die sich freuten
war Licht von außen wie auf einem Teich.

Sie folgte langsam und sie brauchte lang
als wäre etwas noch nicht überstiegen;
und doch: als ob, nach einem Übergang,
sie nicht mehr gehen würde, sondern fliegen.

48

Going Blind

She sat quite like the others there at tea.
It seemed to me at first she grasped her cup
a little differently than the rest.
Once she gave a smile. It almost hurt.

And when people finally stood up and spoke
and slowly and as chance brought it about
moved through many rooms (they talked and laughed),
I saw her. She was moving after the others,

withheld, as one who in a moment
will have to sing and before many people;
upon her bright eyes, that rejoiced,
was light from outside as upon a pool.

She followed slowly, taking a long time,
as though something had not yet been surmounted;
and yet as though, after a crossing over,
she would no longer walk, but fly.

Blaue Hortensie

So wie das letzte Grün in Farbentiegeln
sind diese Blätter, trocken, stumpf und rauh,
hinter den Blütendolden, die ein Blau
nicht auf sich tragen, nur von ferne spiegeln.

Sie spiegeln es verweint und ungenau,
als wollten sie es wiederum verlieren,
und wie in alten blauen Briefpapieren
ist Gelb in ihnen, Violett und Grau;

Verwaschnes wie an einer Kinderschürze,
Nichtmehrgetragnes, dem nichts mehr geschieht:
wie fühlt man eines kleinen Lebens Kürze.

Doch plötzlich scheint das Blau sich zu verneuen
in einer von den Dolden, und man sieht
ein rührend Blaues sich vor Grünem freuen.

Blue Hydrangeas

Like the last green in the palette's colors,
these leaves are without luster, rough and dry
under umbeled flowers that were duller
but for a blue reflected from the sky.

They mirror it, exhausted as with tears,
vaguely, as if not wishing it to stay;
as old blue letter-paper which the years
have touched with yellow, violet, and gray;

washed-out like a child's apron, no more used—
nothing else can happen to it now:
one feels how short the little life has been.

But suddenly the blue seems to renew
itself in one last cluster—and see how
the pathetic blue rejoices in the green.

Vor dem Sommerregen

Auf einmal ist aus allem Grün im Park
man weiß nicht was, ein Etwas, fortgenommen;
man fühlt ihn näher an die Fenster kommen
und schweigsam sein. Inständig nur und stark

ertönt aus dem Gehölz der Regenpfeifer,
man denkt an einen Hieronymus:
so sehr steigt irgend Einsamkeit und Eifer
aus dieser einen Stimme, die der Guß

erhören wird. Des Saales Wände sind
mit ihren Bildern von uns fortgetreten,
als dürften sie nicht hören was wir sagen.

Es spiegeln die verblichenen Tapeten
das ungewisse Licht von Nachmittagen,
in denen man sich fürchtete als Kind.

Before the Summer Rain

Suddenly in the park from all the green,
one knows not what, but something real is gone:
one feels it coming, silent and unseen,
toward the window. Urgently and strong,

out of the wood the dotterel implores —
until one thinks of Saint Jerome: such zeal
and loneliness rise in one voice, which shall
be answered when the rain begins to pour.

Now the walls and pictures of the room
grow dim, as if pushed suddenly away,
as if they dared not hear the words we say.

And on the faded hangings falls the chilled
uncertain light of afternoon: the gloom
in which one felt so frightened, as a child.

Jugend-Bildnis meines Vaters

Im Auge Traum. Die Stirn wie in Berührung
mit etwas Fernem. Um den Mund enorm
viel Jugend, ungelächelte Verführung,
und vor der vollen schmückenden Verschnürung
der schlanken adeligen Uniform
der Säbelkorb und beide Hände—, die
abwarten, ruhig, zu nichts hingedrängt.
Und nun fast nicht mehr sichtbar: als ob sie
zuerst, die Fernes greifenden, verschwänden.
Und alles andre mit sich selbst verhängt
und ausgelöscht als ob wirs nicht verständen
und tief aus seiner eignen Tiefe trüb—.

Du schnell vergehendes Daguerreotyp
in meinen langsamer vergehenden Händen.

Youthful Portrait of My Father

In the eyes dream. The forehead as in touch
with something far. About the mouth enormously
much youth, unsmiled seductiveness,
and before the full ornamental lacings
of the slim aristocratic uniform
the saber's basket-hilt and both the hands —,
that wait, quietly, impelled towards nothing.
And now scarce longer visible: as though they
first, seizers of far things, would disappear.
And all the rest curtained with itself
and effaced, as though we could not understand it,
and clouded deep out of its own depths —.

You swiftly fading daguerreotype
in my more slowly fading hands.

Selbstbildnis aus dem Jahre 1906

Des alten lange adligen Geschlechtes
Feststehendes im Augenbogenbau.
Im Blicke noch der Kindheit Angst und Blau
und Demut da und dort, nicht eines Knechtes
doch eines Dienenden und einer Frau.
Der Mund als Mund gemacht, groß und genau,
nicht überredend, aber ein Gerechtes
Aussagendes. Die Stirne ohne Schlechtes
und gern im Schatten stiller Niederschau.

Das, als Zusammenhang, erst nur geahnt;
noch nie im Leiden oder im Gelingen
zusammgefaßt zu dauerndem Durchdringen,
doch so, als wäre mit zerstreuten Dingen
von fern ein Ernstes, Wirkliches geplant.

Self-Portrait, 1906

The stamina of an old, long-noble race
in the eyebrows' heavy arches. In the mild
blue eyes, the solemn anguish of a child
and, here and there, humility—not a fool's,
but feminine: the look of one who serves.
The mouth quite ordinary, large and straight,
composed, yet not unwilling to speak out
when necessary. The forehead still naive,
most comfortable in shadows, looking down.

This, as a whole, just hazily foreseen—
never, in any joy or suffering,
collected for a firm accomplishment;
and yet, as though, from far off, with scattered Things,
a serious, true work were being planned.

Der König

Der König ist sechzehn Jahre alt.
Sechzehn Jahre und schon der Staat.
Er schaut, wie aus einem Hinterhalt,
vorbei an den Greisen vom Rat

in den Saal hinein und irgendwohin
und fühlt vielleicht nur dies:
an dem schmalen langen harten Kinn
die kalte Kette vom Vlies.

Das Todesurteil vor ihm bleibt
lang ohne Namenszug.
Und sie denken: wie er sich quält.

Sie wüßten, kennten sie ihn genug,
daß er nur langsam bis siebzig zählt
eh er es unterschreibt.

The King

The age of the King is sixteen years.
Sixteen, and already the state.
As though from an ambuscade he peers
past where his grey councillors wait

into the hall and some point therein,
and only feels, maybe,
against his narrow, long, hard chin
the Fleece press chillingly.

Before him the death-warrant they submit
for long remains unsigned.
And they're thinking: It plagues him sore.

They'd know, if they knew enough of his mind,
he's but slowly counting to seventy before
setting his hand to it.

Die Treppe der Orangerie
Versailles

Wie Könige die schließlich nur noch schreiten
fast ohne Ziel, nur um von Zeit zu Zeit
sich den Verneigenden auf beiden Seiten
zu zeigen in des Mantels Einsamkeit —:

so steigt, allein zwischen den Balustraden,
die sich verneigen schon seit Anbeginn,
die Treppe: langsam und von Gottes Gnaden
und auf den Himmel zu und nirgends hin;

als ob sie allen Folgenden befahl
zurückzubleiben, — so daß sie nicht wagen
von ferne nachzugehen; nicht einmal
die schwere Schleppe durfte einer tragen.

The Steps of the Orangery
Versailles

Like worn-out kings who finally slowly stride
without a purpose, only now and then
to show the bowing suite on either side
the loneliness within the mantle's hem:

even so the steps between the balustrades,
which from the very first bowed to the stairs,
climb slowly, also by the grace of God,
toward the sky and lead not anywhere;

as though they had commanded all their horde
to stay far back and not approach again,
even so softly they could not be heard,
nor even dare to bear the heavy train.

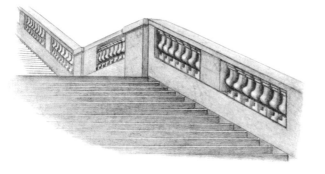

Buddha

Schon von ferne fühlt der fremde scheue
Pilger, wie es golden von ihm träuft;
so als hätten Reiche voller Reue
ihre Heimlichkeiten aufgehäuft.

Aber näher kommend wird er irre
vor der Hoheit dieser Augenbraun:
denn das sind nicht ihre Trinkgeschirre
und die Ohrgehänge ihrer Fraun.

Wüßte einer denn zu sagen, welche
Dinge eingeschmolzen wurden, um
dieses Bild auf diesem Blumenkelche

aufzurichten: stummer, ruhiggelber
als ein goldenes und rundherum
auch den Raum berührend wie sich selber.

Buddha

Unprepared and from afar the traveller
feels the golden radiance drifting from him
as if here in one place many kingdoms,
filled with remorse, had heaped their hidden treasure.

He stares amazed, as he approaches nearer,
at golden eyebrows, lofty and serene —
not at their earrings, ornaments of women,
or dishes, drinking-vessels, tableware.

Who can tell us of the things once melted
down to cast this image and to set it
upright within its calyx — like a flower

richer in stillness, softness, yellowness
than any thing of gold? And everywhere
fully in touch with itself and Space.

Das Karussell
Jardin du Luxembourg

Mit einem Dach und seinem Schatten dreht
sich eine kleine Weile der Bestand
von bunten Pferden, alle aus dem Land,
das lange zögert, eh es untergeht.
Zwar manche sind an Wagen angespannt,
doch alle haben Mut in ihren Mienen;
ein böser roter Löwe geht mit ihnen
und dann und wann ein weißer Elefant.

Sogar ein Hirsch ist da, ganz wie im Wald,
nur daß er einen Sattel trägt und drüber
ein kleines blaues Mädchen aufgeschnallt.

Und auf dem Löwen reitet weiß ein Junge
und hält sich mit der kleinen heißen Hand,
dieweil der Löwe Zähne zeigt und Zunge.

Und dann und wann ein weißer Elefant.

Und auf den Pferden kommen sie vorüber,
auch Mädchen, helle, diesem Pferdesprunge
fast schon entwachsen; mitten in dem Schwunge
schauen sie auf, irgendwohin, herüber—

Und dann und wann ein weißer Elefant.

Und das geht hin und eilt sich, daß es endet,
und kreist und dreht sich nur und hat kein Ziel.
Ein Rot, ein Grün, ein Grau vorbeigesendet,
ein kleines kaum begonnenes Profil—.
Und manchesmal ein Lächeln, hergewendet,
ein seliges, das blendet und verschwendet
an dieses atemlose blinde Spiel...

The Carousel
Jardin du Luxembourg

With a roof and its shadow it rotates
a little while, the herd of particolored
horses, all from the land
that lingers long ere it sinks out of sight.
Some it is true are hitched to carriages,
yet all of them have mettle in their mien;
a vicious red lion goes with them
and every now and then a white elephant.

Even a deer is there quite as in the woods,
save that he bears a saddle and on that
a little blue girl buckled up.

And on the lion rides all white a boy
and holds himself with his small hot hand,
the while the lion shows his teeth and tongue.

And every now and then a white elephant.

And on the horses they come passing by,
girls too, bright girls, who almost have outgrown
this leap of horses; midway in their swing
they look up, anywhere, across—

And every now and then a white elephant.

And this goes on and hurries that it may end,
and only circles and turns and has no goal.
A red, a green, a gray being sent by,
some little profile hardly yet begun.
And occasionally a smile, turning this way,
a happy one, that dazzles and dissipates
over this blind and breathless game.

Die Insel
Nordsee

I
Die nächste Flut verwischt den Weg im Watt,
und alles wird auf allen Seiten gleich;
die kleine Insel draußen aber hat
die Augen zu; verwirrend kreist der Deich

um ihre Wohner, die in einen Schlaf
geboren werden, drin sie viele Welten
verwechseln, schweigend; denn sie reden selten,
und jeder Satz ist wie ein Epitaph

für etwas Angeschwemmtes, Unbekanntes,
das unerklärt zu ihnen kommt und bleibt.
Und so ist alles was ihr Blick beschreibt

von Kindheit an: nicht auf sie Angewandtes,
zu Großes, Rücksichtsloses, Hergesandtes,
das ihre Einsamkeit noch übertreibt.

The Island
North Sea

1
The next high tide will wash away the mud flats'
road, on every side it will look the same;
but out there the little island's
eyes are shut; erratically the dike

surrounds its dwellers, born into
a sleep where they get different
worlds confused, in silence: they hardly ever speak,
and every sentence is like an epitaph

for something washed ashore, something alien
that arrives without explanation and then stays.
And so it is with everything their eyes describe

from childhood on: it's not there because of them,
it's all too huge, too ruthless, sent from somewhere else,
out of proportion even to their loneliness.

II

Als läge er in einem Krater-Kreise
auf einem Mond: ist jeder Hof umdämmt,
und drin die Gärten sind auf gleiche Weise
gekleidet und wie Waisen gleich gekämmt

von jenem Sturm, der sie so rauh erzieht
und tagelang sie bange macht mit Toden.
Dann sitzt man in den Häusern drin und sieht
in schiefen Spiegeln was auf den Kommoden

Seltsames steht. Und einer von den Söhnen
tritt abends vor die Tür und zieht ein Tönen
aus der Harmonika wie Weinen weich;

so hörte ers in einem fremden Hafen —.
Und draußen formt sich eines von den Schafen
ganz groß, fast drohend, auf dem Außendeich.

2

As though it lay within a crater
on a moon, each farm's surrounded by a dike
and inside the gardens are all dressed
the same, like orphans, groomed identically

by the storm that brings them up so harshly,
threatening to kill them day in, day out.
And you sit inside those houses, looking
in crooked mirrors at the odd objects

standing on the chests. And one of the sons
steps outside in the evening and draws a single chord
from a harmonica, like someone quietly weeping;

he heard it played like that once in a foreign harbor.
And out there a tremendous cloud
appears, almost menacing, on the outer dike.

III

Nah ist nur Innres; alles andre fern.
Und dieses Innere gedrängt und täglich
mit allem überfüllt und ganz unsäglich.
Die Insel ist wie ein zu kleiner Stern

welchen der Raum nicht merkt und stumm zerstört
in seinem unbewußten Furchtbarsein,
so daß er, unerhellt und überhört,
allein

damit dies alles doch ein Ende nehme
dunkel auf einer selbsterfundnen Bahn
versucht zu gehen, blindlings, nicht im Plan
der Wandelsterne, Sonnen und Systeme.

3

Only what's inside is near, the rest is far away.
And this interior, crowded, close, everyday,
crammed with everything and beyond describing.
The island's like a shrunken star

which space ignores and soundlessly demolishes
by its unconscious, terrible immensity
so that, unlighted and unseen,
alone,

and only so that this may one day cease,
dark on its own invented course,
it tries to go on, blindly, outside the scheme
of the planets, suns, and galaxies.

Geburt der Venus

An diesem Morgen nach der Nacht, die bang
vergangen war mit Rufen, Unruh, Aufruhr, —
brach alles Meer noch einmal auf und schrie.
Und als der Schrei sich langsam wieder schloß
und von der Himmel blassem Tag und Anfang
herabfiel in der stummen Fische Abgrund —:
gebar das Meer.

Von erster Sonne schimmerte der Haarschaum
der weiten Wogenscham, an deren Rand
das Mädchen aufstand, weiß, verwirrt und feucht.
So wie ein junges grünes Blatt sich rührt,
sich reckt und Eingerolltes langsam aufschlägt,
entfaltete ihr Leib sich in die Kühle
hinein und in den unberührten Frühwind.

Wie Monde stiegen klar die Kniee auf
und tauchten in der Schenkel Wolkenränder;
der Waden schmaler Schatten wich zurück,
die Füße spannten sich und wurden licht,
und die Gelenke lebten wie die Kehlen
von Trinkenden.

Und in dem Kelch des Beckens lag der Leib
wie eine junge Frucht in eines Kindes Hand.
In seines Nabels engem Becher war
das ganze Dunkel dieses hellen Lebens.
Darunter hob sich licht die kleine Welle
und floß beständig über nach den Lenden,
wo dann und wann ein stilles Rieseln war.
Durchschienen aber und noch ohne Schatten,
wie ein Bestand von Birken im April,
warm, leer und unverborgen, lag die Scham.

Birth of Venus

The morning following that fearful night
that passed with shouting, restlessness, and uproar,
the sea burst open yet again and screamed.
And, as the scream ebbed slowly to its close,
and, from the sky's pale daybreak and beginning,
was falling back to the dumb fishes' darkness —
the sea gave birth.

The first rays shimmered on the foaming hair
of the wide wave-vagina, on whose rim
the maiden rose, white and confused and wet.
And, as a young green leaf bestirs itself,
stretches and slowly opens out encurlment,
her body was unfolded into coolness
and into the unfingered wind of dawn.

Like moons the knees went climbing clearly upwards
to dive into the cloud-brims of the thighs;
the narrow shadow of the calves retreated,
the feet extended and grew luminous,
and all the joints became as much alive
as drinkers' throats.

And in the pelvis-chalice lay the belly,
like a young fruit within a childish hand.
And there, within its navel's narrow goblet,
was all this limpid life contained of darkness.
Thereunder lightly rose the little swell
and lapped continually towards the loins
where now and then a silent trickle glistened.
Translucent, though, and still without a shadow,
lay, like a group of silver birch in April,
warm, empty, all-unhidden, the vagina.

Jetzt stand der Schultern rege Waage schon
im Gleichgewichte auf dem graden Körper,
der aus dem Becken wie ein Springbrunn aufstieg
und zögernd in den langen Armen abfiel
und rascher in dem vollen Fall des Haars.

Dann ging sehr langsam das Gesicht vorbei:
aus dem verkürzten Dunkel seiner Neigung
in klares, waagrechtes Erhobensein.
Und hinter ihm verschloß sich steil das Kinn.

Jetzt, da der Hals gestreckt war wie ein Strahl
und wie ein Blumenstiel, darin der Saft steigt,
streckten sich auch die Arme aus wie Hälse
von Schwänen, wenn sie nach dem Ufer suchen.

Dann kam in dieses Leibes dunkle Frühe
wie Morgenwind der erste Atemzug.
Im zartesten Geäst der Aderbäume
entstand ein Flüstern, und das Blut begann
zu rauschen über seinen tiefen Stellen.
Und dieser Wind wuchs an: nun warf er sich
mit allem Atem in die neuen Brüste
und füllte sie und drückte sich in sie,—
daß sie wie Segel, von der Ferne voll,
das leichte Mädchen nach dem Strande drängten.

So landete die Göttin.

Hinter ihr,
die rasch dahinschritt durch die jungen Ufer,
erhoben sich den ganzen Vormittag
die Blumen und die Halme, warm, verwirrt,
wie aus Umarmung. Und sie ging und lief.

And now the shoulders' mobile balance hung
in equipoise upon the wand-straight body,
which mounted from the pelvis like a fountain,
and in the long arms lingeringly descended,
and swiftlier in the hair's abundant fall.

Then, very slowly came the face's progress,
from the fore-shortened dimness of its drooping
into clear horizontal exaltation,
brought to abrupt conclusion by the chin.

Now, when the neck was stretched out like a jet
and like a flower-stalk where sap is mounting,
the arms began to stretch out too, like necks
of swans, when they are making for the shore.

Then entered the dim dawning of this body,
like matutinal wind, the first deep breath.
Within the tenderest branches of the vein-trees
a whispering arose, and then the blood
began to rustle over deeper places.
And this wind grew and grew, until it hurtled
with all its power of breath at the new breasts
and filled them up and forced itself within them,
and they, like filled sails full of the horizon,
impelled the lightsome maiden to the shore.

And thus the goddess landed.

And behind her,
who swiftly left behind the youthful shores,
kept springing up throughout the whole forenoon
the flowers and the grasses, warm, confused,
as from embracing. And she walked and ran.

Am Mittag aber, in der schwersten Stunde,
hob sich das Meer noch einmal auf und warf
einen Delphin an jene selbe Stelle.
Tot, rot und offen.

At noontide, though, in that most heavy hour,
the sea rose up yet once again and flung
a dolphin out upon that self-same spot.
Dead, red, and open.

Die Rosenschale

Zornige sahst du flackern, sahst zwei Knaben
zu einem Etwas sich zusammenballen,
das Haß war und sich auf der Erde wälzte
wie ein von Bienen überfallnes Tier;
Schauspieler, aufgetürmte Übertreiber,
rasende Pferde, die zusammenbrachen,
den Blick wegwerfend, bläkend das Gebiß
als schälte sich der Schädel aus dem Maule.

Nun aber weißt du, wie sich das vergißt:
denn vor dir steht die volle Rosenschale,
die unvergeßlich ist und angefüllt
mit jenem Äußersten von Sein und Neigen,
Hinhalten, Niemals-Gebenkönnen, Dastehn,
das unser sein mag: Äußerstes auch uns.

Lautloses Leben, Aufgehn ohne Ende,
Raum-brauchen ohne Raum von jenem Raum
zu nehmen, den die Dinge rings verringern,
fast nicht Umrissen-sein wie Ausgespartes
und lauter Inneres, viel seltsam Zartes
und Sich-bescheinendes — bis an den Rand:
ist irgend etwas uns bekannt wie dies?

Und dann wie dies: daß ein Gefühl entsteht,
weil Blütenblätter Blütenblätter rühren?
Und dies: daß eins sich aufschlägt wie ein Lid,
und drunter liegen lauter Augenlider,
geschlossene, als ob sie, zehnfach schlafend,
zu dämpfen hätten eines Innern Sehkraft.
Und dies vor allem: daß durch diese Blätter
das Licht hindurch muß. Aus den tausend Himmeln
filtern sie langsam jenen Tropfen Dunkel,
in dessen Feuerschein das wirre Bündel
der Staubgefäße sich erregt und aufbäumt.

The Bowl of Roses

You've seen the flare of anger, seen two boys
bunch themselves up into a ball of something
that was mere hate and roll upon the ground
like a dumb animal attacked by bees;
actors, sky-towering exaggerators,
the crashing downfall of careering horses,
casting away their sight, flashing their teeth
as though the skull were peeling from the mouth.

But now you know how such things are forgotten;
for now before you stands the bowl of roses,
the unforgettable, entirely filled
with that extremity of being and bending,
proffer beyond all power of giving, presence,
that might be ours: that might be our extreme.

Living in silence, endless opening out,
space being used, but without space being taken
from that space which the things around diminish;
absence of outline, like untinted groundwork
and mere Within; so much so strangely tender
and self-illumined — to the very verge: —
where do we know of anything like this?

And this: a feeling able to arise
through petals being touched by other petals?
And this: that one should open like an eyelid,
and lying there beneath it simply eyelids,
all of them closed, as though they had to slumber
ten-fold to quench some inward power of vision.
And this, above all: that through all these petals
light has to penetrate. From thousand heavens
they slowly filter out that drop of darkness
within whose fiery glow the mazy bundle
of stamens stirs itself and reaches upwards.

Und die Bewegung in den Rosen, sieh:
Gebärden von so kleinem Ausschlagswinkel,
daß sie unsichtbar blieben, liefen ihre
Strahlen nicht auseinander in das Weltall.

Sieh jene weiße, die sich selig aufschlug
und dasteht in den großen offnen Blättern
wie eine Venus aufrecht in der Muschel;
und die errötende, die wie verwirrt
nach einer kühlen sich hinüberwendet,
und wie die kühle fühllos sich zurückzieht,
und wie die kalte steht, in sich gehüllt,
unter den offenen, die alles abtun.
Und *was* sie abtun, wie das leicht und schwer,
wie es ein Mantel, eine Last, ein Flügel
und eine Maske sein kann, je nach dem,
und *wie* sie's abtun: wie vor dem Geliebten.

Was können sie nicht sein: war jene gelbe,
die hohl und offen daliegt, nicht die Schale
von einer Frucht, darin dasselbe Gelb,
gesammelter, orangeröter, Saft war?
Und wars für diese schon zu viel, das Aufgehn,
weil an der Luft ihr namenloses Rosa
den bittern Nachgeschmack des Lila annahm?
Und die batistene, ist sie kein Kleid,
in dem noch zart und atemwarm das Hemd steckt,
mit dem zugleich es abgeworfen wurde
im Morgenschatten an dem alten Waldbad?
Und diese hier, opalnes Porzellan,
zerbrechlich, eine flache Chinatasse
und angefüllt mit kleinen hellen Faltern, —
und jene da, die nichts enthält als sich.

And then the movement in the roses, look:
gestures deflected through such tiny angles,
they'd all remain invisible unless
their rays ran streaming out into the cosmos.

Look at that white one, blissfully unfolded
and standing in the great big open petals
like Venus upright in her mussel shell;
look how that blusher there, as in confusion,
has turned towards a cooler bloom, and how
the cool one is unfeelingly withdrawing;
and how the cold one stands, wrapped in herself,
among those open roses doffing all.
And *what* they doff — the way it can appear
now light, now heavy — like a cloak, a burden,
a wing, a domino — it all depends —
and *how* they doff it: as before the loved one.

What can they *not* be: was that yellow one
that lies there hollow, open, not the rind
upon a fruit, in which that self-same yellow
was the intenser, orange-ruddier juice?
And did her blowing prove too much for this one,
since, touched by air, her nameless rosiness
assumed the bitter after-taste of lilac?
And is not yonder cambric one a dress,
wherein, still soft and breath-warm, clings the vest
flung off along with it among the shadows
of early morning by the woodland pool?
And what's this opalescent porcelain,
so fragile, but a shallow china cup,
and full of little shining butterflies?
And that, containing nothing but herself?

Und sind nicht alle so, nur sich enthaltend,
wenn Sich-enthalten heißt: die Welt da draußen
und Wind und Regen und Geduld des Frühlings
und Schuld und Unruh und vermummtes Schicksal
und Dunkelheit der abendlichen Erde
bis auf der Wolken Wandel, Flucht und Anflug,
bis auf den vagen Einfluß ferner Sterne
in eine Hand voll Innres zu verwandeln.

Nun liegt es sorglos in den offnen Rosen.

And are not all just that, just self-containing,
if self-containing means: to take the world
and wind and rain and patience of the spring-time
and guilt and restlessness and muffled fate
and sombreness of evening earth and even
the melting, fleeing, forming of the clouds
and the vague influence of distant stars,
and change it to a handful of Within?

It now lies heedless in those open roses.

BUCH 2 | BOOK 2

Archaïscher Torso Apollos

Wir kannten nicht sein unerhörtes Haupt,
darin die Augenäpfel reiften. Aber
sein Torso glüht noch wie ein Kandelaber,
in dem sein Schauen, nur zurückgeschraubt,

sich hält und glänzt. Sonst könnte nicht der Bug
der Brust dich blenden, und im leisen Drehen
der Lenden könnte nicht ein Lächeln gehen
zu jener Mitte, die die Zeugung trug.

Sonst stünde dieser Stein entstellt und kurz
unter der Schultern durchsichtigem Sturz
und flimmerte nicht so wie Raubtierfelle;

und bräche nicht aus allen seinen Rändern
aus wie ein Stern: denn da is keine Stelle,
die dich nicht sieht. Du mußt dein Leben ändern.

Archaic Torso of Apollo

We cannot know his legendary head
with eyes like ripening fruit. And yet his torso
is still suffused with brilliance from inside,
like a lamp, in which his gaze, now turned to low,

gleams in all its power. Otherwise
the curved breast could not dazzle you so, nor could
a smile run through the placid hips and thighs
to that dark center where procreation flared.

Otherwise this stone would seem defaced
beneath the translucent cascade of the shoulders
and would not glisten like a wild beast's fur:

would not, from all the borders of itself,
burst like a star: for here there is no place
that does not see you. You must change your life.

Leda

Als ihn der Gott in seiner Not betrat,
erschrak er fast, den Schwan so schön zu finden;
er ließ sich ganz verwirrt in ihm verschwinden.
Schon aber trug ihn sein Betrug zur Tat,

bevor er noch des unerprobten Seins
Gefühle prüfte. Und die Aufgetane
erkannte schon den Kommenden im Schwane
und wußte schon: er bat um Eins,

das sie, verwirrt in ihrem Widerstand,
nicht mehr verbergen konnte. Er kam nieder
und halsend durch die immer schwächre Hand

ließ sich der Gott in die Geliebte los.
Dann erst empfand er glücklich sein Gefieder
und wurde wirklich Schwan in ihrem Schooß.

Leda

When the god in his great need crossed inside,
he was shocked almost to find the swan so beautiful;
he slipped himself inside it all confused.
But his deceit bore him toward the deed

before he'd put that untried being's
feelings to the test. And the opened woman
saw at once who was coming in the swan
and understood: he asked *one* thing

which she, confused in her resistance,
no longer could hold back. The god came down
and necking through the ever weaker hand

released himself into the one he loved.
Then only he felt his feathers with delight,
and grew truly swan within her womb.

Delphine

Jene Wirklichen, die ihrem Gleichen
überall zu wachsen und zu wohnen
gaben, fühlten an verwandten Zeichen
Gleiche in den aufgelösten Reichen,
die der Gott, mit triefenden Tritonen,
überströmt bisweilen übersteigt;
denn da hatte sich das Tier gezeigt:
anders als die stumme, stumpfgemute
Zucht der Fische, Blut von ihrem Blute
und von fern dem Menschlichen geneigt.

Eine Schar kam, die sich überschlug,
froh, als fühlte sie die Fluten glänzend:
Warme, Zugetane, deren Zug
wie mit Zuversicht die Fahrt bekränzend,
leichtgebunden um den runden Bug
wie um einer Vase Rumpf und Rundung,
selig, sorglos, sicher vor Verwundung,
aufgerichtet, hingerissen, rauschend
und im Tauchen mit den Wellen tauschend
die Trireme heiter weitertrug.

Und der Schiffer nahm den neugewährten
Freund in seine einsame Gefahr
und ersann für ihn, für den Gefährten,
dankbar eine Welt und hielt für wahr,
daß er Töne liebte, Götter, Gärten
und das tiefe, stille Sternenjahr.

90

Dolphins

Those so real, who in such diverse places
credited their like with growth and dwelling,
came to feel through some akinning traces
likenesses within the liquid spaces
which the god, with Triton train upwelling,
would bestride all-overstreamingly;
for the creature showed there suddenly:
different from the dumbly-vegetating
fishy kind — with their own blood pulsating,
and with yearnings for humanity.

Somersaulting came a school one day,
glad as though they felt the waves' resplendence:
warm and closely-clinging, whose array,
garlanding the voyage with self-dependence,
round the curving prow in loose relay
like some swelling vase's foliation,
happy, care-free, safe from laceration,
leaping up erect, enraptured, surging,
changing with the billows in submerging,
bore the trireme cheerly on its way.

And the sailor took the new-presented
friend on his lone perilous career,
and for his companion there invented
gratefully a world, which his own dear
sounds and gods and gardens elemented
and the deeply-silent stellar year.

Legende von den drei Lebendigen und den drei Toten

Drei Herren hatten mit Falken gebeizt
und freuten sich auf das Gelag.
Da nahm sie der Greis in Beschlag
und führte. Die Reiter hielten gespreizt
vor dem dreifachen Sarkophag,

der ihnen dreimal entgegenstank,
in den Mund, in die Nase, ins Sehn;
und sie wußten es gleich: da lagen lang
drei Tote mitten im Untergang
und ließen sich gräßlich gehn.

Und sie hatten nur noch ihr Jägergehör
reinlich hinter dem Sturmbandlör;
doch da zischte der Alte sein:
— Sie gingen nicht durch das Nadelöhr
und gehen niemals — hinein.

Nun blieb ihnen noch ihr klares Getast,
das stark war vom Jagen und heiß;
doch das hatte ein Frost von hinten gefaßt
und trieb ihm Eis in den Schweiß.

The Legend of the Three Living and the Three Dead Men

Three falconers, three hungry lords
anxious to feast, rode home.
An old man led them through the wood
until their horses shied and reared
before the triple tomb.

A threefold stench offended
each nose and mouth and eye —
within, they could not doubt it,
three long-dead bodies lay
dissolving in decay.

Under the leather riding-hoods
the falconers' ears, still keen,
heard the words the old man whispered:
They could not pass through the needle's eye,
they cannot enter in.

Their falconers' hands stayed firm and warm,
their hearts beat fast from the chase,
but a cold blight followed the hunters home
and it chilled their sweat to ice.

Das jüngste Gericht

So erschrocken, wie sie nie erschraken,
ohne Ordnung, oft durchlocht und locker,
hocken sie in dem geborstnen Ocker
ihres Ackers, nicht von ihren Laken

abzubringen, die sie liebgewannen.
Aber Engel kommen an, um Öle
einzuträufeln in die trocknen Pfannen
und um jedem in die Achselhöhle

das zu legen, was er in dem Lärme
damals seines Lebens nicht entweihte;
denn dort hat es noch ein wenig Wärme,

daß es nicht des Herren Hand erkälte
oben, wenn er es aus jeder Seite
leise greift, zu fühlen, ob es gälte.

The Last Judgment

Shocked as they were never shocked before,
in no apparent order, many full of holes
or coming apart, they squat there in the ruptured
ochre of their fields, and cling

to the shrouds they've grown fond of.
But angels arrive, bringing oil
to trickle into desiccated sockets
and to place under each armpit

a belonging they'd somehow neglected
to desecrate during a whole lifetime's uproar;
for there it can still get a little warmth,

so that it doesn't chill the Lord's hand
up above, when he gathers it from every side
gently, to see if it's worth anything.

Die Versuchung

Nein, es half nicht, daß er sich die scharfen
Stacheln einhieb in das geile Fleisch;
alle seine trächtigen Sinne warfen
unter kreißendem Gekreisch

Frühgeburten: schiefe, hingeschielte
kriechende und fliegende Gesichte,
Nichte, deren nur auf ihn erpichte
Bosheit sich verband und mit ihm spielte.

Und schon hatten seine Sinne Enkel;
denn das Pack war fruchtbar in der Nacht
und in immer bunterem Gesprenkel
hingehudelt und verhundertfacht.
Aus dem Ganzen ward ein Trank gemacht:
seine Hände griffen lauter Henkel,
und der Schatten schob sich auf wie Schenkel
warm und zu Umarmungen erwacht—.

Und da schrie er nach dem Engel, schrie:
Und der Engel kam in seinem Schein
und war da: und jagte sie
wieder in den Heiligen hinein,

daß er mit Geteufel und Getier
in sich weiterringe wie seit Jahren
und sich Gott, den lange noch nicht klaren,
innen aus dem Jäsen destillier.

The Temptation

No, it didn't help, that he drove sharp
thorns into his lecherous flesh;
all his pregnant senses threw forth
amid shrill laboring shrieking

half-cocked births: lopsided, leeringly envisaged
crawling and flying apparitions,
nothings, whose malice, bent on him alone,
united and had fun with him.

And already his senses had grandchildren:
for the pack was fruitful in the night
and in wilder and wilder specklings
botched itself and multiplied by hundreds.
From the whole mix a drink was made:
his hands grasped sheer handles,
and the shadows slid open like thighs
warm and wakened for embracing—.

And then he screamed for the angel, screamed:
And the angel came in his halo
and was present: and drove them
back inside the saint again,

that he might wrestle on within himself
with beasts and demons as for years now
and make God, the as yet far from clear,
out of the ferment inwardly distill.

Der Reliquienschrein

Draussen wartete auf alle Ringe
und auf jedes Kettenglied
Schicksal, das nicht ohne sie geschieht.
Drinnen waren sie nur Dinge, Dinge
die er schmiedete; denn vor dem Schmied
war sogar die Krone, die er bog,
nur ein Ding, ein zitterndes und eines
das er finster wie im Zorn erzog
zu dem Tragen eines reinen Steines.

Seine Augen wurden immer kälter
von dem kalten täglichen Getränk;
aber als der herrliche Behälter
(goldgetrieben, köstlich, vielkarätig)
fertig vor ihm stand, das Weihgeschenk,
daß darin ein kleines Handgelenk
fürder wohne, weiß und wundertätig:

blieb er ohne Ende auf den Knien,
hingeworfen, weinend, nichtmehr wagend,
seine Seele niederschlagend
vor dem ruhigen Rubin,
der ihn zu gewahren schien
und ihn, plötzlich um sein Dasein fragend,
ansah wie aus Dynastien.

The Reliquary

Outside there awaited all the rings,
every chain-link, destiny
which without them could not come to be.
Inside they were only things, just things
which he worked; for, plying his artistry,
even the crown he twisted would appear
just a thing, a trembling thing alone,
which, as grimly as in rage, he'd rear
for the wearing of a purest stone.

And his eyes were growing ever-colder
from the cold diurnal compotation;
when, though, all complete, the glorious holder
(heavily engilded, sumptuous)
stood before him, ripe for consecration,
destined for the future habitation
of a small hand, white, miraculous:

long then he remained upon his knees,
prostrate, weeping, daring now no more,
lowering his soul before
the quiet ruby, by which he's
being noticed, as he thinks he sees,
and, with sudden asking what he's for,
gazed at as from dynasties.

Adam

Staunend steht er an der Kathedrale
steilem Aufstieg, nah der Fensterrose,
wie erschreckt von der Apotheose,
welche wuchs und ihn mit einem Male

niederstellte über die und die.
Und er ragt und freut sich seiner Dauer
schlicht entschlossen; als der Ackerbauer
der begann, und der nicht wußte, wie

aus dem fertig-vollen Garten Eden
einen Ausweg in die neue Erde
finden. Gott war schwer zu überreden;

und er drohte ihm, statt zu gewähren,
immer wieder, daß er sterben werde.
Doch der Mensch bestand: sie wird gebären.

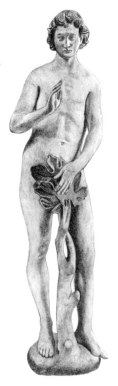

Adam

Marveling he stands on the cathedral's
steep ascent, close to the rose window,
as though frightened at the apotheosis
which grew and all at once

set him down over these and these.
And straight he stands and glad of his endurance,
simply determined; as the husbandman
who began and who knew not how

from the garden of Eden finished-full
to find a way out into
the new earth. God was hard to persuade;

and threatened him, instead of acceding,
ever and again, that he would die.
Yet man persisted: she will bring forth.

Eva

Einfach steht sie an der Kathedrale
großem Aufstieg, nah der Fensterrose,
mit dem Apfel in der Apfelpose,
schuldlos-schuldig ein für alle Male

an dem Wachsenden, das sie gebar,
seit sie aus dem Kreis der Ewigkeiten
liebend fortging, um sich durchzustreiten
durch die Erde, wie ein junges Jahr.

Ach, sie hätte gern in jenem Land
noch ein wenig weilen mögen, achtend
auf der Tiere eintracht und Verstand.

Doch da sie den Mann entschlossen fand,
ging sie mit ihm, nach dem Tode trachtend;
und sie hatte Gott noch kaum gekannt.

Eve

Simply she stands on the cathedral's
great ascent, close to the rose window,
with the apple in the apple-pose,
guiltless-guilty once and for all

of the growing she gave birth to
since from the circle of eternities
loving she went forth, to struggle through
her way throughout the earth like a young year.

Ah, gladly yet a little in that land
would she have lingered, heeding the harmony
and understanding of the animals.

But since she found the man determined,
she went with him, aspiring after death,
and she had as yet hardly known God.

Schwartze Katze

Ein Gespenst ist noch wie eine Stelle,
dran dein Blick mit einem Klange stößt;
aber da, an diesem schwarzen Felle
wird dein stärkstes Schauen aufgelöst:

wie ein Tobender, wenn er in vollster
Raserei ins Schwarze stampft,
jählings am benehmenden Gepolster
einer Zelle aufhört und verdampft.

Alle Blicke, die sie jemals trafen,
scheint sie also an sich zu verhehlen,
um darüber drohend und verdrossen
zuzuschauern und damit zu schlafen.
Doch auf einmal kehrt sie, wie geweckt,
ihr Gesicht und mitten in das deine:
und da triffst du deinen Blick im geelen
Amber ihrer runden Augensteine
unerwartet wieder: eingeschlossen
wie ein ausgestorbenes Insekt.

Black Cat

A ghost, though invisible, still is like a place
your sight can knock on, echoing; but here
within this thick black pelt, your strongest gaze
will be absorbed and utterly disappear:

just as a raving madman, when nothing else
can ease him, charges into his dark night
howling, pounds on the padded wall, and feels
the rage being taken in and pacified.

She seems to hide all looks that have ever fallen
into her, so that, like an audience,
she can look them over, menacing and sullen,
and curl up to sleep with them. But all at once

as if awakened, she turns her face to yours;
and with a shock, you see yourself, tiny,
inside the golden amber of her eyeballs
suspended, like a prehistoric fly.

Landschaft

Wie zuletzt, in einem Augenblick
aufgehäuft aus Hängen, Häusern, Stücken
alter Himmel und zerbrochnen Brücken,
und von drüben her, wie vom Geschick,
von dem Sonnenuntergang getroffen,
angeschuldigt, aufgerissen, offen —
ginge dort die Ortschaft tragisch aus:

fiele nicht auf einmal in das Wunde,
drin zerfließend, aus der nächsten Stunde
jener Tropfen kühlen Blaus,
der die Nacht schon in den Abend mischt,
so daß das von ferne Angefachte
sachte, wie erlöst, erlischt.

Ruhig sind die Tore und die Bogen,
durchsichtige Wolken wogen
über blassen Häuserreihn
die schon Dunkel in sich eingesogen;
aber plötzlich ist vom Mond ein Schein
durchgeglitten, licht, als hätte ein
Erzengel irgendwo sein Schwert gezogen.

Townscape

All at once, piles of heaped-up buildings
and escarpments and the broken fragments
of the ancient skies, the shattered bridges,
unprotected and exposed, lie threatened
by the orange flames of sunset—
the whole city sentenced to destruction
as if fate had destined it for this:

then a touch of blue, like healing lotion
twilight mixed with darkness might provide,
bathes the wound and, later, softly quenching,
cools the angry fire which the sun
has already kindled; leaves the town
quiet and at peace, as if reprieved.

Empty colonnades and silent gateways.
Vast translucent cloudbanks billow
over streets whose pallid houses
wait in rows and drink the darkness.
Suddenly a shaft of moonlight
shines out fiercely, as if somewhere
the archangel had unsheathed his brilliant sword.

Römische Campagna

Aus der vollgestellten Stadt, die lieber
schliefe, träumend von den hohen Thermen,
geht der grade Gräberweg ins Fieber;
und die Fenster in den letzten Fermen

sehn ihm nach mit einem bösen Blick.
Und er hat sie immer im Genick,
wenn er hingeht, rechts und links zerstörend,
bis er draußen atemlos beschwörend

seine Leere zu den Himmeln hebt,
hastig um sich schauend, ob ihn keine
Fenster treffen. Während er den weiten

Aquädukten zuwinkt herzuschreiten,
geben ihm die Himmel für die seine
ihre Leere, die ihn überlebt.

Roman Campagna

Out of the cluttered city which would rather
doze, dreaming of the lofty thermal springs,
smoothly the road of tombs descends in fever;
from the last farm the windows' glittering

follows the roadway with an evil look.
And the road has them always at his neck
as he goes down, destroying right and left,
till breathlessly, imploringly, he lifts

his very emptiness toward the sky,
glancing about him quickly, on the sly,
to see if any window still is spying.

And while he beckons the broad aqueducts
to come, the skies return as usufruct
for his small emptiness theirs which survive him.

Papageien-Park

Jardin des Plantes, Paris

Unter türkischen Linden, die blühen, an Rasenrändern,
in leise von ihrem Heimweh geschaukelten Ständern
atmen die Ara und wissen von ihren Ländern,
die sich, auch wenn sie nicht hinsehn, nicht verändern.

Fremd im beschäftigten Grünen wie eine Parade,
zieren sie sich und fühlen sich selber zu schade,
und mit den kostbaren Schnäbeln aus Jaspis und Jade
kauen sie Graues, verschleudern es, finden es fade.

Unten klauben die duffen Tauben, was sie nicht mögen,
während sich oben die höhnischen Vögel verbeugen
zwischen den beiden fast leeren vergeudeten Trögen.

Aber dann wiegen sie wieder und schläfern und äugen,
spielen mit dunkelen Zungen, die gerne lögen,
zerstreut an den Fußfesselringen. Warten auf Zeugen.

The Parrot House
Jardin des Plantes, Paris

Under the flowering limes at the edge of the lawns,
balanced on perches that silently rock with their yearning
they breathe in the alien air, always remembering
their homeland; distant, unseen and forever unchanging.

Too precious for everyday life in the trees, as exotic,
as foreign, as actors, they preen and attend to their costumes;
exquisite beaks fashioned of jade and of jasper
chew on the tasteless grey stuff they deliberately squander.

Below them, pedestrian pigeons peck up what lies scattered,
while they scornfully stoop between troughs
with little or nothing left in them, the contents rejected.

They go back to their brooding; rocking and leering; letting
livid tongues, dark and mendacious, absently
play with the chains of their shackles: wait for their audience.

Bildnis

Daß von dem verzichtenden Gesichte
keiner ihrer großen Schmerzen fiele,
trägt sie langsam durch die Trauerspiele
ihrer Züge schönen welken Strauß,
wild gebunden und schon beinah lose;
manchmal fällt, wie eine Tuberose,
ein verlornes Lächeln müd heraus.

Und sie geht gelassen drüber hin,
müde, mit den schönen blinden Händen,
welche wissen, daß sie es nicht fänden, —

und sie sagt Erdichtetes, darin
Schicksal schwankt, gewolltes, irgendeines,
und sie giebt ihm ihrer Seele Sinn,
daß es ausbricht wie ein Ungemeines:
wie das Schreien eines Steines —

und sie läßt, mit hochgehobnem Kinn,
alle diese Worte wieder fallen,
ohne bleibend; denn nicht eins von allen
ist der wehen Wirklichkeit gemäß,
ihrem einzigen Eigentum,
das sie, wie ein fußloses Gefäß,
halten muß, hoch über ihren Ruhm
und den Gang der Abende hinaus.

Portrait

Unwilling that the look of self-denial
should tell the whole world of her private sorrows,
she holds the faded posy of her features
(artlessly bound and now fatigued and pale)
attentively through the long tragedies —
but sometimes like a single tuberose
a smile is lost from it, escapes and falls:

she passes negligently over it,
weary and, with her lovely sightless hands
knowing they never can recover it, resigned

she speaks her lines (the fickleness of fate,
contrived and commonplace) enriching all,
expressing the uniqueness of her heart
offering her own extraordinary soul:
the grief, the lamentation of a stone!

She lets the words fall from her upraised face
content to let them pass; for none of them
can measure up to raw reality
which stays her only true possession
and which, like a vase without a base,
she is obliged to carry constantly
with her — lifting it high above her fame,
above the evenings moving in procession.

San Marco
Venedig

In diesem Innern, das wie ausgehöhlt
sich wölbt und wendet in den goldnen Smalten,
rundkantig, glatt, mit Köstlichkeit geölt,
ward dieses Staates Dunkelheit gehalten

und heimlich aufgehäuft, als Gleichgewicht
des Lichtes, das in allen seinen Dingen
sich so vermehrte, daß sie fast vergingen —.
Und plötzlich zweifelst du: vergehn sie nicht?

und drängst zurück die harte Galerie,
die, wie ein Gang im Bergwerk, nah am Glanz
der Wölbung hängt; und du erkennst die heile

Helle des Ausblicks: aber irgendwie
wehmütig messend ihre müde Weile
am nahen Überstehn des Viergespanns.

San Marco
Venice

In this interior which, as excavated,
arches and twists within the golden foil,
round-cornered, glistening as with precious oil,
this city's darkness was accommodated

and secretly heaped up to balance out
that overplus of brightness, so pervading
all her possessions they were almost fading. —
And 'Aren't they fading?' comes the sudden doubt;

and, thrusting back the minish gallery
suspended near the vaulting's golden gleam,
you hail the unimpaired illumination

of that wide view; yet somehow mournfully
measuring its fatigued continuation
with that of the adjacent four-horse team.

Corrida

In memoriam Montez, 1830

Seit er, klein beinah, aus dem Toril
ausbrach, aufgescheuchten Augs und Ohrs,
und den Eigensinn des Picadors
und die Bänderhaken wie im Spiel

hinnahm, ist die stürmische Gestalt
angewachsen — sieh: zu welcher Masse,
aufgehäuft aus altem schwarzen Hasse,
und das Haupt zu einer Faust geballt,

nicht mehr spielend gegen irgendwen,
nein: die blutigen Nackenhaken hissend
hinter den gefällten Hörnern, wissend
und von Ewigkeit her gegen Den,

der in Gold und mauver Rosaseide
plötzlich umkehrt und, wie einen Schwarm
Bienen und als ob ers eben leide,
den Bestürzten unter seinem Arm

durchläßt, — während seine Blicke heiß
sich noch einmal heben, leichtgelenkt,
und als schlüge draußen jener Kreis
sich aus ihrem Glanz und Dunkel nieder
und aus jedem Schlagen seiner Lider,

ehe er gleichmütig, ungehässig,
an sich selbst gelehnt, gelassen, lässig
in die wiederhergerollte große
Woge über dem verlornen Stoße
seinen Degen beinah sanft versenkt.

Corrida
In Memoriam Montez, 1830

Since, small almost, through the opened door
with upstartled eyes and ears he came
and supposed the baiting picador
and beribboned barbs to be a game,

that wild figure seems now to consist
of an ever-concentrating weight
of accumulated old black hate,
and his head is clenched into a fist,

no more meeting any playfully:
no, but rearing bloody barbs behind
those presented horns, and in his mind
his opponent from eternity,

who, in gold and mauve-pink silk arrayed,
suddenly turns round and, like a swarm
of bees, and as if vexed but undismayed,
lets the baffled beast beneath his arm

rush by,—while his burning looks are lifting
up once more in tremulous accord,
as if all that circling throng were drifting
down from their own shine and sombering
and his eyelids' every fluttering,

till, so unexcitedly, unhating,
leaning on himself, deliberating,
into that great wave's refluctuance
over its dispersed precipitance
almost softly he insheathes his sword.

Übung am Klavier

Der Sommer summt. Der Nachmittag macht müde;
sie atmete verwirrt ihr frisches Kleid
und legte in die triftige Etüde
die Ungeduld nach einer Wirklichkeit,

die kommen konnte: morgen, heute abend —,
die vielleicht da war, die man nur verbarg;
und vor den Fenstern, hoch und alles habend,
empfand sie plötzlich den verwöhnten Park.

Da brach sie ab; schaute hinaus, verschränkte
die Hände; wünschte sich ein langes Buch —
und schob auf einmal den Jasmingeruch
erzürnt zurück. Sie fand, daß er sie kränkte.

Piano Practice

Summer buzzes through the drowsy mood
of afternoon. Confused, she fluffs her fresh
dress, and into the profound étude
she plays impatiently a fretfulness

for something real that might befall tomorrow,
this evening, or perhaps now in the dark
is hidden. Suddenly through the lofty window
she is aware of the richly pampered park.

She breaks off playing, looks out, twines her hands,
wishes for some long book, and then, disturbed,
she pushes back the jasmine scent. She finds
the fragrance hurts.

Dame vor dem Spiegel

Wie in einem Schlaftrunk Spezerein
löst sie leise in dem flüssigklaren
Spiegel ihr ermüdetes Gebaren;
und sie tut ihr Lächeln ganz hinein.

Und sie wartet, daß die Flüssigkeit
davon steigt; dann gießt sie ihre Haare
in den Spiegel und, die wunderbare
Schulter hebend aus dem Abendkleid,

trinkt sie still aus ihrem Bild. Sie trinkt,
was ein Liebender im Taumel tränke,
prüfend, voller Mißtraun; und sie winkt

erst der Zofe, wenn sie auf dem Grunde
ihres Spiegels Lichter findet, Schränke
und das Trübe einer späten Stunde.

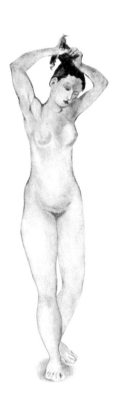

Lady Before the Mirror

At the mirror's surface she'll begin
gently melting, like a spice-assortment
in a sleeping draught, her tired deportment;
and she'll let her smiling drop right in.

And she'll wait until the liquidness
rises from it; then she'll pour her hair
in as well, and, lifting out one bare,
marvellous shoulder from her evening-dress,

quietly drink out her image. Drink,
what a lover would in wild caresses,
tryingly, all mistrust; and never think

of beckoning her maid until she sees
at the mirror's bottom candles, presses,
and a late hour's undissolving lees.

Die Sonnenuhr

Selten reicht ein Schauer feuchter Fäule
aus dem Gartenschatten, wo einander
Tropfen fallen hören und ein Wander-
vogel lautet, zu der Säule,
die in Majoran und Koriander
steht und Sommerstunden zeigt;

nur sobald die Dame (der ein Diener
nachfolgt) in dem hellen Florentiner
über ihren Rand sich neigt,
wird sie schattig und verschweigt—.

Oder wenn ein sommerlicher Regen
aufkommt aus dem wogenden Bewegen
hoher Kronen, hat sie eine Pause;
denn sie weiß die Zeit nicht auszudrücken,
die dann in den Frucht- und Blumenstücken
plötzlich glüht im weißen Gartenhause.

The Sundial

Seldom any shower of damp putrescence
from the garden shadow, where the falling
drops can hear themselves, and there's one calling
migratory bird, can reach the presence
of that marjoram and coriander-
circled stone, with summer hours to show:

save when, soon as she, whom an attendant
always follows, in her widely pendent
bright straw hat inclines too low,
it's obscured and doesn't know;

or when, on a summer rain's emergence
from the lofty tree-top's wild insurgence,
it becomes entitled to repose;
since to tell that time exceeds its powers
which within the painted fruits and flowers
in the white pavilion then upglows.

Schlaf-Mohn

Abseits im Garten blüht der böse Schlaf,
in welchem die, die heimlich eingedrungen,
die Liebe fanden junger Spiegelungen,
die willig waren, offen und konkav,

und Träume, die mit aufgeregten Masken
auftraten, riesiger durch die Kothurne—:
das alles stockt in diesen oben flasken
weichlichen Stengeln, die die Samenurne

(nachdem sie lang, die Knospe abwärts tragend,
zu welken meinten) festverschlossen heben:
gefranste Kelche auseinanderschlagend,
die fieberhaft das Mohngefäß umgeben.

Opium Poppy

In beds apart those baneful slumbers wave,
where some, contriving secret enterings,
have found the love of youthful mirrorings,
that proved most willing, open, and concave,

and dreams that in excited masks came trooping
on with a stature buskinedly imposing: —
it's all congealed within those topward drooping,
tenuous stalks, which, after long supposing,

with their bowed buds, that they were withering,
uplift the tight-shut seed-urns on their shoulders:
unfurling all the frilly petalling
that feverishly surrounds the poppy-holders.

Die Flamingos

Jardin des Plantes, Paris

In Spiegelbildern wie von Fragonard
ist doch von ihrem Weiß und ihrer Röte
nicht mehr gegeben, als dir einer böte,
wenn er von seiner Freundin sagt: sie war

noch sanft von Schlaf. Denn steigen sie ins Grüne
und stehn, auf rosa Stielen leicht gedreht,
beisammen, blühend, wie in einem Beet,
verführen sie verführender als Phryne

sich selber; bis sie ihres Auges Bleiche
hinhalsend bergen in der eignen Weiche,
in welcher Schwarz und Fruchtrot sich versteckt.

Auf einmal kreischt ein Neid durch die Volière;
sie aber haben sich erstaunt gestreckt
und schreiten einzeln ins Imaginäre.

The Flamingos

Paris, Jardin des Plantes

Like mirrored images by Fragonard,
so little of their red and white is shown,
and delicately, as if one came alone
and whispered of his mistress in your ear:

She lay there, flushed with sleep.... Above the green
reeds they rise and on their rose-stilts turn,
blooming together, as if on a parterre,
seducing (more seductively than Phryne)

themselves; and in the softness where the black
and apple-red are veiled they sink their necks,
hiding the pallid circles of their eyes,

till through their wire cage swift envy shrieks;
they waken in astonishment and stretch
themselves and soar imaginary skies.

Persisches Heliotrop

Es könnte sein, daß dir der Rose Lob
zu laut erscheint für deine Freundin: Nimm
das schön gestickte Kraut und überstimm
mit dringend flüsterndem Heliotrop

den Bülbül, der an ihren Lieblingsplätzen
sie schreiend preist und sie nicht kennt.
Denn sieh: wie süße Worte nachts in Sätzen
beisammenstehn ganz dicht, durch nichts getrennt,
aus der Vokale wachem Violett
hindüftend durch das stille Himmelbett—:

so schließen sich vor dem gesteppten Laube
deutliche Sterne zu der seidnen Traube
und mischen, daß sie fast davon verschwimmt,
die Stille mit Vanille und mit Zimmt.

Persian Heliotrope

It may be that the beauty of the rose
seems much too flagrant, that it seems too loud
to celebrate and sing your mistress' praise:
this flower's embroidered subtlety exceeds

the bulbul's love-song singing in her bowers
to serenade her though it does not know her.
Like words by night in whispered messages,
urgent and dense, no silences between,
a violet whispering of voices sends
its fragrance to perfume the attentive heavens

and, lucent stars affixed to silken berries,
the blossom shines against its latticed leaves
breathing a sweet intoxicating potion:
silence spiced with vanilla, cinnamon.

Schlaflied

Einmal wenn ich dich verlier,
wirst du schlafen können, ohne
daß ich wie eine Lindenkrone
mich verflüstre über dir?

Ohne daß ich hier wache und
Worte, beinah wie Augenlider,
auf deine Brüste, auf deine Glieder
niederlege, auf deinen Mund.

Ohne daß ich dich verschließ
und dich allein mit Deinem lasse
wie einen Garten mit einer Masse
von Melissen und Stern-Anis.

Lullaby

Someday if I lose you,
how will you sleep without
my whispering above you
like the linden's branches?

Without my lying here
awake and placing words, almost
like eyelids, on your breasts,
your limbs, your lips.

Without my closing you
and leaving you alone with what is yours
like a garden with a mass
of mint-balm and star-anise.

Rosa Hortensie

Wer nahm das Rosa an? Wer wußte auch,
daß es sich sammelte in diesen Dolden?
Wie Dinge unter Gold, die sich entgolden,
entröten sie sich sanft, wie im Gebrauch.

Daß sie für solches Rosa nichts verlangen.
Bleibt es für sie und lächelt aus der Luft?
Sind Engel da, es zärtlich zu empfangen,
wenn es vergeht, großmütig wie ein Duft?

Oder vielleicht auch geben sie es preis,
damit es nie erführe vom Verblühn.
Doch unter diesem Rosa hat ein Grün
gehorcht, das jetzt verwelkt und alles weiß.

Pink Hydrangea

Who could have guessed this pink? And who could know
that it would gather here within these clusters? —
Their colour gradually fades away,
as gold on gilded things wears out through use.

There is no charge. No payment is required.
Does pink endure to smile down from on high?
Shall there be Angels, welcoming and tender,
when, prodigal as scent, it has to die?

But maybe they simply let it fall,
perhaps to spare it from its withering.
Beneath the pink a green, forever listening
and withering already, now knows all.

Der Leser

Wer kennt ihn, diesen, welcher sein Gesicht
wegsenkte aus dem Sein zu einem zweiten,
das nur das schnelle Wenden voller Seiten
manchmal gewaltsam unterbricht?

Selbst seine Mutter wäre nicht gewiß,
ob *er* es ist, der da mit seinem Schatten
Getränktes liest. Und wir, die Stunden hatten,
was wissen wir, wieviel ihm hinschwand, bis

er mühsam aufsah: alles auf sich hebend,
was unten in dem Buche sich verhielt,
mit Augen, welche, statt zu nehmen, gebend
anstießen an die fertig-volle Welt:
wie stille Kinder, die allein gespielt,
auf einmal das Vorhandene erfahren;
doch seine Züge, die geordnet waren,
blieben für immer umgestellt.

The Reader

Who knows this stranger who has turned his face
away from life to live another life —
which nothing interrupts except the swift
and forceful turning of each printed page?

Even a mother might not recognise
her son, lost in the world that lies below him,
steeped in his own shadow. What can we know —
who live our lives so governed by mere hours —

of other lives he may have lived and lost
before he looks up, heavy now and burdened
with all the matter which his book contains?
As children rise from play and look around
his eyes now turn to all that lies outside,
towards the world again made manifest;
but yet his face, for all its discipline,
will never while he lives change back again.

Der Apfelgarten
Borgeby-Gård

Komm gleich nach dem Sonnenuntergange,
sieh das Abendgrün des Rasengrunds;
ist es nicht, als hätten wir es lange
angesammelt und erspart in uns,

um es jetzt aus Fühlen und Erinnern,
neuer Hoffnung, halbvergeßnem Freun,
noch vermischt mit Dunkel aus dem Innern,
in Gedanken vor uns hinzustreun

unter Bäume wie von Dürer, die
das Gewicht von hundert Arbeitstagen
in den überfüllten Früchten tragen,
dienend, voll Geduld, versuchend, wie

das, was alle Maße übersteigt,
noch zu heben ist und hinzugeben,
wenn man willig, durch ein langes Leben
nur das Eine will und wächst und schweigt.

The Apple Orchard

Borgeby gård

Come when the sun has set and you shall see
the green of evening stain the grassy ground:
how easily we might believe that we
ourselves had tended it and sown,

so that in present feeling and remembering
of new-born hopes, of half-forgotten joys
seasoned with darker feelings deep within,
we could believe we now spread out before us

the heavy harvest of a hundred days
beneath old trees that Dürer might have drawn
which stand there silent, serving, seeking ways
to bear the fruits which weigh their branches down;

to raise and proffer what grows, measureless,
for those who long and patiently endure —
who all their lives sustaining their desire
for one thing only, silently increase.

Der Berg

Sechsunddreißig Mal und hundert Mal
hat der Maler jenen Berg geschrieben,
weggerissen, wieder hingetrieben
(sechsunddreißig Mal und hundert Mal)

zu dem unbegreiflichen Vulkane,
selig, voll Versuchung, ohne Rat, —
während der mit Umriß Angetane
seiner Herrlichkeit nicht Einhalt tat:

tausendmal aus allen Tagen tauchend,
Nächte ohne gleichen von sich ab
falen lassend, alle wie zu knapp;
jedes Bild im Augenblick verbrauchend,
von Gestalt gesteigert zu Gestalt,
teilnahmslos und weit und ohne Meinung —,
um auf einmal wissend, wie Erscheinung,
sich zu heben hinter jedem Spalt.

The Mountain

Thirty-six times, then a hundred times,
conjuring the mountain to his page,
driven back to it then dragged away
thirty-six times then a hundred times,

he turns to the volcano yet again
joyful, mesmerised, yet unsuccessful,
trying like a madman in his line
to capture the unrepresentable . . .

Judging them imperfect, insufficient,
it lets nights unequalled slip away
reappearing on a thousand days
to exploit each image in its moment;
letting each manifestation grow,
generous, impartial, unconcerned,
knowing at once as though by revelation
how to show its face at every window.

Der Hund

Da oben wird das Bild von einer Welt
aus Blicken immerfort erneut und gilt.
Nur manchmal, heimlich, kommt ein Ding und stellt
sich neben ihn, wenn er durch dieses Bild

sich drängt, ganz unten, anders, wie er ist;
nicht ausgestoßen und nicht eingereiht,
und wie im Zweifel seine Wirklichkeit
weggebend an das Bild, das er vergißt,

um dennoch immer wieder sein Gesicht
hineinzuhalten, fast mit einem Flehen,
beinah begreifend, nah am Einverstehen
und doch verzichtend: denn er wäre nicht.

The Dog

A world of image is what counts — up there —
and is continually renewed by sight.
Yet sometimes some *thing* secretly comes near,
stays by him as he seeks to penetrate

beyond the image — like himself, apart,
inferior and, fundamentally,
though not excluded yet kept separate.
Unsure, he gives the image his reality

and then, forgetting, none the less
holds up his face to it beseechingly
and, nearly satisfied, nearly accepts
but still rejects it — for he could not *be*.

Der Käferstein

Sind nicht Sterne fast in deiner Nähe
und was giebt es, das du nicht umspannst,
da du dieser harten Skarabäe
Karneolkern gar nicht fassen kannst

ohne jenen Raum, der ihre Schilder
niederhält, auf deinem ganzen Blut
mitzutragen; niemals war er milder,
näher, hingegebener. Er ruht

seit Jahrtausenden auf diesen Käfern,
wo ihn keiner braucht und unterbricht;
und die Käfer schließen sich und schläfern
unter seinem wiegenden Gewicht.

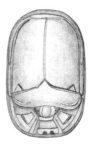

The Scarab

Surely the stars are not so far distant
and there is little you do not possess
each time you take the scarab in your hand;
whose hard, cornelian heart encompasses

the *space* which presses down and firms its scales
and, never more accessible or gentler,
enters the blood, accompanies and fills.
Forever near them, for millennia

never made use of and left undisturbed
it hangs above the scarabs as they rest,
dreaming, locked up inside themselves, secure,
and rocking in the cradle of its heaviness.

Buddha in der Glorie

Mitte aller Mitten, Kern der Kerne,
Mandel, die sich einschließt und versüßt, —
dieses Alles bis an alle Sterne
ist dein Fruchtfleisch: Sei gegrüßt.

Sieh, du fühlst, wie nichts mehr an dir hängt;
im Unendlichen ist deine Schale,
und dort steht der starke Saft und drängt.
Und von außen hilft ihm ein Gestrahle,

denn ganz oben werden deine Sonnen
voll und glühend umgedreht.
Doch in dir ist schon begonnen,
was die Sonnen übersteht.

Buddha in Glory

Center of all centers, core of cores,
almond self-enclosed and growing sweet—
all this universe, to the furthest stars
and beyond them, is your flesh, your fruit.

Now you feel how nothing clings to you;
your vast shell reaches into endless space,
and there the rich, thick fluids rise and flow.
Illuminated in your infinite peace,

a billion stars go spinning through the night,
blazing high above your head.
But *in* you is the presence that
will be, when all the stars are dead.

ABOUT THE TRANSLATORS

Stephen Cohn's translations of Rainer Maria Rilke's poetry include the *Duino Elegies* and *New Poems*.

Richard Exner's translations of various Rilke poems appeared in the English translation of a biography of Rainer Maria Rilke by Wolfgang Leppmann.

Albert Ernest Flemming's translation of *Rainer Maria Rilke: Selected Poems* culminated a lifetime's reading and reflection on Rilke's poetry.

J. B. Leishman's translations of Rainer Maria Rilke's poetry include *Requiem and Other Poems, Duino Elegies* (with Stephen Spender), *Sonnets to Orpheus, From the Remains of Count C. W., Poems 1906–1926, Later Poems,* and *Selected Works: Poetry.*

C. F. MacIntyre's translations of Rainer Maria Rilke's poetry include *Duino Elegies, The Life of the Virgin Mary, Sonnets to Orpheus,* and *Selected Poems.*

Stephen Mitchell's translations of Rainer Maria Rilke's poetry include *Duino Elegies, Sonnets to Orpheus, Letters to a Young Poet, The Notebooks of Malte Laurids Brigge, Ahead of All Parting: The Selected Poetry and Prose of Rainer Maria Rilke,* and *Last Poems.*

M. D. Herter Norton was the translator of many volumes of Rainer Maria Rilke's poetry, including *Letters to a Young Poet, Sonnets to Orpheus, Wartime Letters to Rainer Maria Rilke, The Lay of the Love and Death of Cornet Christopher Rilke, The Notebooks of Malte Laurids Brigge,* and *Stories of God*.

Edward Snow is the translator of many volumes of Rainer Maria Rilke's poetry, including *New Poems (1907), New Poems: The Other Part (1908), The Book of Images,* and *Uncollected Poems.*

Franz Wright's translations first appeared in Rainer Maria Rilke's *The Unknown Rilke: Expanded Edition,* Field Translation Series 17, Oberlin College Press.

TRANSLATION CREDITS

"Epitaph for a Young Girl," "Pietà," "The Rose Window," "The Poet," "Buddha" (page 63), "The Legend of the Three Living and the Three Dead Men," "Townscape," "The Parrot House," "Portrait," "Persian Heliotrope," "Pink Hydrangea," "The Reader," "The Apple Orchard," "The Mountain," "The Dog," and "The Scarab" reprinted from *Rilke: New Poems,* translated by Stephen Cohn © 1992 by permission of the publisher, Carcanet Press Limited.

"The Panther" from *Rilke: A Life,* by Wolfgang Leppmann, verse translation by Richard Exner, translation copyright © 1984 by Fromm International Publishing Corporation, New York. Reprinted with permission of Fromm International Publishing Corporation.

"Early Apollo" and "The Angel of the Meridian" reprinted from *Rainer Maria Rilke: Selected Poems,* translated by Albert Ernest Flemming © 1983 by permission of the publisher, Routledge: New York and London.

"Buddha" (page 21), "The Cathedral," "Morgue," "The Unicorn," "Roman Sarcophagi," "The King," "Birth of Venus," "The Bowl of Roses," "Dolphins," "The Reliquary," "San Marco," "Corrida," "Lady Before the Mirror," "The Sundial," and "Opium Poppy" by Rainer Maria Rilke, from *New Poems,* translated by J. B. Leishman, copyright © 1964 by The Hogarth Press. Reprinted by permission of New Directions Publishing Corporation.

"The Gazelle," "The Swan," "Blue Hydrangeas," "Before the Summer Rain," "The Steps of the Orangery," "Roman Campagna," "Piano Practice," and "The Flamingos" reprinted from *Selected Poems: Bilingual Edition,* translated/edited by C. F. MacIntyre, copyright © 1940, 1968 by C. F. MacIntyre. Reprinted by permission of the Regents of the University of California and the University of California Press.

ACKNOWLEDGMENTS

I would like to thank Sarah Longacre for photographing a number of the sites and objects in Paris that inspired Rilke's *New Poems,* and Vanessa Longacre for capturing the white elephant. Thanks also to Stephanie Speer and Mary Nikoloric for pictures of Buddha, and Christopher Kuntze for making a coherent design. Many people helped with permissions and proofreading, but specially Karen Dane, without whom this book would not have been possible. Thanks to all.

Ferris Cook
New York City
June 22, 1997

Book design by Christopher Kuntze
Printed by The Stinehour Press, Lunenburg, Vermont
Bound by Acme Bookbinding, Charlestown, Massachusetts